T0068975

ANIMISM

ALSO BY DENNIS SCHMITZ

ANIMISM

DENNIS SCHMITZ

Oberlin College Press
Oberlin, Ohio

The FIELD Poetry Series, vol. 33
Oberlin College Press, 50 N. Professor Street, Oberlin, OH 44074
www.oberlin.edu/ocpress

Cover and book design: Steve Farkas
Cover art: Martín Ramírez (1895-1963), *Untitled (Abstract Patterns with Four Animals)*, 1953. © Copyright Estate of Martín Ramírez. Reproduced by permission.

Library of Congress Cataloging-in-Publication Data

Schmitz, Dennis, 1937-
  [Poems. Selections]
  Animism / Dennis Schmitz.
      pages cm. — (The FIELD Poetry series ; v. 33)
  ISBN 978-0-932440-47-1 (paperback : alk. paper) — ISBN 0-932440-47-9 (paperback : alk. paper)
  I. Title.
  PS3569.C517A6 2014
  811'.54—dc23
                                    2013048338

For Loretta, again & always

For Dan, Sam, Pete, Gordon & Irene

Contents

III

I

Animism

Imagine your favorite CEO furry, forepaws
up, with a nut in his teeth—what if every

bureaucrat & CEO who ruined it were forced
to live in nature? But it is not enough

to make a CEO scamper in a poem,
though the poem seeps water vinegary with

solvents from a shunt creek at the company
outlet. Even if you make the CEO shrug

downstream on his belly, you'll change
nothing. You must believe that the gods inside

things can re-make themselves, that rural houses
will set themselves on fire—though the tree

is cut, the spirit won't leave the wood.
Bless the jay whose dogma is rancorous

but who still absorbs blue heaven.
Bless the 8 AM windfall apples so spattered

that the only solvent for the light is more
of the light that spattered them.

Learning to Swim in the Public Pool

to our son John

You died, a few days old, in an isolette,
but all your supposed childhood, I take you

out & concentrate until you flicker
briefly in specifics. I take you out

cold-water days, acid-rock radio or
country music drained away by wind,

& coax you, your body only imagined
blue & pimply as fresh stucco,

coax you into congruence with water.
Unable to absorb the art by absorbing

the medium itself (the first lesson),
you choke on the water & go down

until your eyes rub darkness,
your ears fill, bubbles thread up

out of every body-opening that squints
to hold you. After a while, your eyes

won't close on the grainy overhead
sunlight through which adult legs kick,

through which their careless hands
slash. Up here, we have 5 PM's caramelized

light. Up here, dry & clothed, we argue
dinner. Up here, other kids queue

along the pool's nicked edge, all profile
like figures in an Egyptian frieze.

Pushing between them, your mother
kneels, wets her lips to whisper down

into the water that Putin will free
the dissidents. Up here I promise

hot-dogs. Up here, the tired lifeguard's
hiccups thin to breathing. The hardest

lesson is to want to come up again.

Bird-Talk

Their beaks tell you what they feed on:
needle probes trees for bugs,

blunt-beak breaks seeds.
What about Tina, newly-divorced, wiping

her beak as she hauls her laundry,
stamping emotional hunger down

our shared backstairs?
The sparrow, seed-geek, calls

out the size of what it discards
until it discards even its call.

Tina's overheard *sotto voce* is
a loose fit for every bird-

emotion except wrath, which humans
can will, probably first in nouns,

or the verbs which help us
measure our inadequate stools or the meds

like grief we weep late night into a pillow,
thus, we hope, discarding them.

Bats

too must translate their lovers
from a limbo of night-objects—

heels up, they sleep off their intimacy.
But life intends a bat to eat flies

that all day shimmer on barnyard waste,
& at night drift in spoken clouds

the bat eats as it scrubs its bitten,
bloodied fur against poultry wire to get them.

A bat's cry is the tiniest of human sounds.
But however human the cry, the tongue is only

a caul thought is born with. The poem itself
is a bat that mistakes its love—a poem utters

its small pain until another's body answers.

Intimacy

Sometimes intimacy only means no elsewhere:
that June I dutifully read *The Golden Bowl*,

swaying to & from the job on the crowded
Lake Street el, at first bored then repelled

by Adam Verver's incestuous clinging.
Every night I'd tear fifteen pages more,

staple them into a throwaway daily reading
of love's duplicities. Days, I wrapped toys

at Goldblatt's, my touch sticky
where I'd glued shut paper cuts or thumbed

snakes of tape around gift toys
while Chicago's impatient moms or dads elbowed

each other into frenzy. On the el-ride
home, Verver bought his daughter an Italian

prince or the shopman wrapped
our novelist's flawed golden bowl into

a symbol, sure to break later.
All around me cramped passengers shook

in & out of pairs; basted with one another's
sweats, they tried not to look at faces,

but I read faces while I used James
to fend off a heavy woman in stiletto

heels as she wobbled in & out of libidinal
balance. Someone behind me wanted to tear

off my shirt. A man cursed in two languages.
Intimacy makes its heat by friction—

some of us just smolder, some burn.

The Synopsis of a Novel

is also a novel, like the bad one which begins: *Jocelyn*
rode the horse until her thighs ached & her attention

rode, indifferently, her tired body....
Of course, you keep the humans, & later they crush

the bed's chenille spread. On the floor, Jocelyn's purse
is still inside out, but spilling fewer coins & folded bills.

A shorter rain will pock the puddles when she more quickly
leaves—but if you've written her love too small,

how do you keep this Jocelyn & focus the wrung-out
light in the trees, & keep too the important potatoes

sending out white feelers in the kitchen bin?

The Woods

The wolf from an adjacent story
would pursue him if the dwarf didn't,

but at last the feverish child
is asleep, & as you inadvertently open

your mouth against the animal
& flower pattern on the child's bed-sheet

against which you too lie, but inaccurate
& too big, you too begin to breathe your way

into sleep. Fever is switchbacks
& sweaty going, uphill—even a cough

loosens the leaves on the trees
until you must redo the dream for which

awake-life is only a displacement.
Breathe deeper into the sheet—in your sweat

& spit, the laundered-out animals come
back wet but vivid as you restlessly turn

to print your eye into the foliage.
This way is the trail—that way,

blackened with sleep, the woods.

Listening to Pan

Music is a complex belief system
with a simple god—
it is all innuendo like a dog's bark,

like the dog I walk
nightly who barks at what's far back
in Bullen Wood, who is still wild
enough to hear *wild* even in a caged bird's

misquote. The dog is like the Senegalese
drummer that scientists, defeated by the nature
of song, hired. Though the scientists

tried to sing or moan
with the whales, they couldn't hear,
couldn't isolate even one whale's virtuosity

from the whales' taped chatter
until the hired drummer, used to finding
his rhythm in an ensemble

of players, heard. Tonight my dog hears
only his own fear. I hear the clarinet
in "Forbidden Love" as my parents foxtrot

once more & I watch from a remembered
bedroom. The record is worn
from desire's play & replay, & the dancers fade.

Come back, I say *sotto
voce*, leaves wetting my forehead as I look
deeper into the Wood, the dog restless—come back.
But it is cold & the dog doesn't believe.

Our Place

Our size, somewhere between actual
Antares & its night-sky dot.

Our love a nibbling, somewhere between
a black bear's appetite & the smallest

eater that solved the fence's
fir posts except where a tin patch

shimmers & ferns glow.
Against a shredded log we lay our clothes

for ants to eat out what itches.
Another hunger: a hand's breadth across

a small birthmark, above your bare
shoulder, your hair shimmers, undisturbed.

Our place is also this summer rental,
this August when we live under laurels

which themselves twist for sun
under redwoods. This August is long;

the tarpaper roof steams & the torn grass.
Greedy sweat gathers the down under

your pinned hair, twisted back
for comfort. But comfort is the last thing

one wants from love. Comfort is an affliction
that gathers jewels like the grease in the drain

of stones shines where you spilled it.

Phone Calls

Thought is first a nail-point coming
down, an obsession, but *talk* is

what two humans hammer
down into a new off-deck entrance,

the dwelling each wants in a marriage.
The storm-door glass each looks

through to see the other rattles
on the catch. After husband # 2,

Lydia bought a Doberman,
kept its muzzle bloody-spattered

with red aniline dye to demonstrate
vicarious ferocity. High on solvents,

the dog ripped through screen & door
both to Jack coming back 4 PM

for clothes. Who was bestial & who talked
mongrel need? Her late-night return

calls were for love, she said.
Not for *talk*, but for *thought,*

each hammered at the other's head.

Film Noir

Widmark's famous cackle as he pushes
another crook's mother in her wheelchair

down the tenement stairs, or Bogart lisping love
to Bacall, saying his "forever" but subtracting

some of the "forever" she had pledged
to her husband. Film noir's dawn is always

porcelain chipped black
at the basin's lip. In the real 1940s,

who knew? & anyway, the facts of love
could be misunderstood, as Mrs. Tschigfrei,

our upstairs renter, hinted, paying my mother,
the three of us standing there, Mrs. T's cane

pawing the porch-boards near my toes
as she leaned her smell closer, her husband

too embarrassed by his own injuries
to face my mother. I stepped away then

from Mrs. T's cane, & a few months later,
the Tschigfreis too moved. Children can learn

a movie kind of irony as my mother had
learned to distance Mrs. T's few dollars

from what Mrs. T was paying for.

Picking Blackberries

Your own children bite your hands
to get at any fruit you pick, Farney's mother,

our guide, warned about families, her voice
out of cadence with her hands, more knowing

than ours, quicker children's hands.
Mother, we thought, nodded as she picked.

Later, Mother sent us into deeper
thickets from which the three of us never

looked back to the crawl-holes.
Our shredded clothes were spotted with

juice or bleeding, our voices unhappily
plasmic with berry-pulp as we screamed

to each other the insults jays utter,
mistaking other species for their own.

How clever jays seem, how like humans.
Washed down with a sunlight tangled

in bugs, the jays feed, heads tilted, alert.

Talking into the Monster's Hat

but not daring to wear it, I'd whisper
let me be your Igor, talking to the Nazi

who'd worn the hat all my childhood ago,
a Frankenstein my uncle tried not to be

in a war he'd fought until he'd finished,
liking beer too much, tight-lipped about

deaths for which he'd volunteered.
The hero version has my bloodied uncle take

the hat from the head of the man he's killed.
But it's a Wehrmacht dress hat, the Nazi

buff or collector I sold it to sighed, & not
the Luftwaffe hat your ad said. Your uncle,

he said, bought it with cigarettes from his opposite
in the long line of the Nazi uninjured that

films show us. Or the hat was trophy from Alps
of captured stuff the Allies bulldozed as the first step

to German forgetting. See how all of us play
at the evil, rub ourselves in it, eat it second-hand

in spit-up—which metaphor says enough—
dipped in fixative, my uncle flapped & writhed

on a pin of conscience? Or, my favorite image,
the prancing Igor of the movie, who, dropping it,

almost stepping on it, finally gets the bad brain
back into Frankenstein's lab basin?

Tarzan

in the movies, a wild human improbably raised
by apes—I remember my own mother's nervous

preening, the ticks she'd prize from my scalp's
tangle. Our movie Tarzan, howling Johnny

Weissmuller, broke his nose when his vine swung
him into an elephant's butt. Going away to college,

I sat for hours in an elm tree's fork, telling my hands
to close around the vine. How does one find peace

in the jungle—the broken toothpaste tube, Jane's
drying pantyhose noodling down from a towel-bar?

What do the ads say, what do the Sufis, the I Ching
recommend? *If I cease to desire & remain still,*

the Empire will be at peace of its own accord....
The poet Allen Ginsberg, a Tarzan of free love,

loved the Hindu holy men who swept the jungle
dirt ahead of themselves not to step on any life.

The Historic Shot Tower

field trip I hated was third grade;
the fabled mangle & tubs of the convent

laundry were second. Our nuns led us,
but a tower guide with wounds

painted on his torn Civil War dress-up
told, a little excited, a little loud,

just how well the old technology
killed. & we took turns inside the empty

tower seeing up where the sky percolated
Iowa's sulfurous October weather.

I saw nothing an eight-year-old could lift—
the rusted & unwieldy smelting gear,

lead from local mines the Indians had cursed,
or the thousands dead—can a child

unlearn war? War for us was a bloodied
nose at recess, & the elaborate postwar

shaming was with our nun finding the words
the bully then mumbled in front of class.

Dungeon—Sutter's Fort, CA

The straw is smelly, but our bodies
smell more—sweat-maps about

the armpits & loins where we cross
other bodies the chains bend us

to, sometimes on the face
another's face or the repulsive

ornament the rapist showed
in the Bosch painting of DESIRE.

Victims scarred with kisses,
we slide out of reach—the crooked

horse-dealer, or typecast Injun
Joes, maybe any randy

pioneer once a month
with camp whores choosing hatred

over loneliness because each day
decomposed where the next one grew.

Some farms were rich swamps
that a summer sun stunned,

or, north, volcanic outcroppings
pinched roots & nothing ripened.

Whatever we planted,
fingers knotted around what we knew,

children came up foreign,
wives came up dead—home was

a word the wind ate. Now this cellar
memory makes—over it some tried

to build, but underneath, the old bodies
are condemned, me to you.

Heckfire

for Georgia & Death Penalty Focus

Though the nuns forgave us, we taught
ourselves guilt—Farney & I only

tardy but sent to the school's furnace-
room, sentenced to Heckfire, to look at

our souls somehow burned visible but gassy
in the coals as our janitor swung the furnace-

door with his shovel, pinholes of red going
out on his big hands. He was wronged king

or Luther to the Catholic 3rd grade,
though he stank of pee or his lunch beer

Farney dared sip a few grades later.

Is there a kind of higher janitor for killers,
a holiest pope or mahatma to pick

up barehanded the soul's splintery blue
acetylene flame that cuts or mends metal

when the alloy for God-ness is beaten thin
& digressive to make evil?

The CNN reporter is groomed but rigid by the prisoner's wheel-
chair. 25 years after his crime, the latest California killer is
legally blind & dying, but his reprieve, the reporter says, is denied.

Vengeance is a lazy kind of grieving,
the translator says later in the HBO movie

(she's relaxed now & earnest)—
the victim's family in this tribe takes

the killer far out in a boat & leaves him
in the water—they can choose to let him

drown or begin the hard work of forgiving
him by bringing him up wet & afraid.

Song of Myself

Who gets the god's drink pure & who gets
just a sip diluted with spit or human sobs

only Heifitz could've played into a Paganini
encore? I'm taping up my torn Whitman,

already crackly with tape, in more tape
as I metaphorically rewrap the Clark St. bookstall

where Whitman was wedged with thrillers
& Harlequins. I began writing my bad Whitman

in the book next to his, riding the Lake St. el &
trembling because each person on the train expected

the poem-word that would turn away suicide
or cure flaccid love. I was exultant too

with the train at third-floor level past
grimed stock-rooms & secretaries maybe

flustered their first time in poems, but their faces
lit with nuance thanks to my inadequate Whitman.

Seldom a *camerado*, never an *imperturbe*,
I'd channel Whitman in my Chicago cold-water flat,

its wallpaper pimply with roaches
I'd smashed impasto & gritty with crockery pieces.

I chanted Whitman until my breath was
a runny glue of whispers. Then, in the shower's

hot clouds to ease congestion, linoleum slick,
I'd be a tenor, his lips in a memorized zero,

with all his 300 lbs squeezing out "addio."
But drinking water out of the toilet or barking

at other strays doesn't make you a dog;
you can't *learn* levitation—only Whitman

was Whitman.

Yellowjackets

dispute in a bag they make
of wood & insect spit; humans buzz

inside gossip any two can chew
from a shared brioche with latte

as its suffix. We are so many
that our wings can't beat open

even if the bag is big
as Iraq (Bush, even Bin Laden

have tiny wings), the body-counted
like all the eyes in tapioca laboriously

spooned out for fussy children's appetites.
We chew Koran, Bible or Torah,

but whatever we pray still comes out buzz.

Brand Loyalty

Alka-Seltzer works nicely as an internal
decontaminant, while a paste of Tide and corn
meal is an excellent agent to cleanse radioactive
waste from the skin. —Robert C. Ricks, Oak Ridge, TN

The two-minute TV close-up shows how
your wife & you can coat each other's faces,

smooth your grins to fetal calmness.
With your hands, you trowel on the damp
mush, incidentally caressing as you do.

Its grit is ur-white, a snow of detergent—
if Russia is still the enemy, it's Siberia
that's an eye-stinging white, a plaster

of sentry-boxes & shaved heads—
the taste-enhancers, the additives
which could kill you if you had time

to live into cancer, save you now.
Only those may live who almost died
in the kitchen, or who were caught keeping
warm in the all-night grocery when
its ten-foot window rippled with aftershock.

After you coat each other, you coat
your children with products the ads sold you,
a parody of brand loyalty.
If only you could spit back what kept you

alive, cover where you metaphorically scar
with a poultice, a pasty guilt that slides
over the child's undeveloped nipple
into the umber navel-knot which the family

dog sniffs, at which he whines, smelling death.

Accidents & Effects

Accidents in the Aristotelian sense means that
my Basque friend Constantine would not have died

anyway from the rattlesnake. *Bite* is secondary
in the definition of snake—so why did his father

slap him & call Constantine stupid for running uphill
(pumping *effects* faster), berry canes biting at him,

shredding his new shirt, the really small rattlesnake
swinging by tiny fangs from his wrist?

When our German neighbor died in a car
accident, the will defined one of her *effects*

as a stuffed Chihuahua she'd called Aunt Tilly's dog.
Mt. St. Helens, erupting, blew Washington ash-*effects*

hubcap deep for downtown Portland, Oregon drivers,
but no one died. Of those protesting death at Rancho Seco

nuclear reactor's possible *accident*, who would've done
the probable dying? One sly protestor released helium

balloons printed with just the words *nuclear-effects,*
which were picked up months later in Washington & Idaho.

The Last Judgment

Under the Sistine Chapel roof, God dried
before Michelangelo could define Him

with sin's alizarins & chalky blues.
Above the altar, the bad dead

wait more patiently than the good.
The art of it forces us to cramp

back our necks more, guilty of something
we aren't allowed to know

here below, elbows in, body-surfing
the tourist crowds in Rome's worst July.

Then it's noon & the Pope's cops shoo
all of us back too early through

the vestment museum, the chained-off
satellite chapels, driving us

deprived of our yearning,
down the 16th-century small-person stairs.

Because even religion must eat lunch,
we are driven out of heaven—

chiuso to Lutherans, AIDS victims,
single mothers & Nazis. *Chiuso*

to the lumpish, dark-skinned woman
in a sari, its saffron coating

the slick last stairs Loretta & I help
her down—*closed*, the guard insists

in English—all of us pushed out
into the Viale Vaticano's rainy

dead-end, tourists.

Doppelganger

or just a somnambulistic self,
a Denny who does the grunt-work

while I sleep—wiping out rust rings
on the glass shelf, picking hair out

of the toothbrushes, the cleanser grit,
the stain on porcelain a cigarette burned—

absorbing, always absorbing. Mornings,
I postulate a dangerous, occult envy;

the cleaned mirror consuming my face
in reprisal, the pants-leg wrinkles—

everything, even the love-broken mattress,
re-shaping to my body's attrition.

My Grandfather's Gambol

Now only the dresser mirror watches
Grandfather, barefoot & suspenders

down, begin his beguine, twisting
& flicking his head the way birds do

when they drink. As he re-swallows
the first rest-home months,

his union-suit buttons ripple.
He shuffles what Cole Porter he can,

& when he sings, it's a grandma
he won't bring back peevish—

not yet a paean or hymn,
but the introductory throat-clearing

before God enters the music, & words
swerve to correct our feelings

or re-make Eden. The farm was
a Depression loss, Adam's bit-open love

offered between the couple.
In town, he'll live arthritic & long,

a two-job death.

On the Mercator Map

but from nearby Berkeley, our Anne
phones dog-news first. I am stubble-faced

& sleepy. She says Greenland is a mental
terrain, logistically untrue, she says, & only

stretched so that Europe will lie flat.
I know that she will take me back next, as I took

her then, finger to finger through difficult Africa.
She was six & so bright—our globe was a wet

pebbled orange with Africa on one side,
South America on the other. I'd inked Sao Paulo

on the orange's skin, & Dakar, like the eyes
on either side of a horse's head, independent

& separate visions, even if (before continental
drift) the Amazon had run, inches deep,

over a green Sahara. I'd cut the skin away
whole, my knife making the Mercator map

show distortion of surface, that surface itself
is an idea we throw away in order to eat the inside—

the juice, overflowing our lips as we talked,
had dotted the tablecloth.

Thirteen

years old all Saturday tossed
father's tennis-ball, its nap barely

whirring the flaked ceiling paint
but never marking the ceiling, never

asserting the ball-shape against father's
rules, never penetrating the blue-

paint-heaven lit only by a dim
100W (it's day & the boy is punished).

Sometimes a thirteen-year-old
body has nap all over the haunted kinks,

the new muscle. The object of the game
is to harness gravity, hold the ball up

there until your head hurts, then let
the ball (after it brushes the blue) fall,

watching it come down, & without
flinching, let it come down & thud

exactly off your forehead at the same
time as it thuds inside your head.

Quid Pro Quo

My uncle, nightshift at Westmark Meats,
at first mistakes his own for the animal's

body, in the cold, cuts himself & not it—
just experimental nicks but enough.

Wobbly after standing ten hours reaching
up arm-deep into dozens of bodies

without heads or feet, my uncle appreciates
quid pro quo & stands another hour on his porch

when he comes home. The light left on
all night for him drinks color until the elms

are achromatic, washed out. There his Alsatian
trembles for affection & whines as my uncle

touches him, senses with the dog where the dog's
joints break & the fatty hide covers deep places.

Boundaries We Don't See

The farm's boundary should be
a seasonal creek, but here's barbwire

so rusted into the October thicket that color
alone can't define it. It's only talk

my brother & I take turns carrying
as, with the owner's permission, we step

off the legal description of our father's
boyhood farm, so many times re-sold—

someone else's implement-shed,
the barn in the thirties photo now white.

A pole too limber, the station sign too high—
only an attendant, he tries to change the prices

of gas. Sweating, in his chair too long,
& a continent away, trying not to do it,

the driver of the Predator drone flies it
into an Afghan wedding party.

Belief like the rust on barbwire,
I pray past it. Next in line at the reliquary,

I kneel to kiss whatever is left
of the saint.

III

Bait

Light like a corrosive wiped
across the sky, 6 AM—Crawford's pond

is obsolete before we have time
to find it in a moonscape of half-decided

condos, the rust & yellow trencher,
its claw down in burdock & snapped

alder, skids of 2x4s, skids
of greenish waferboard: Crawford's

secret, his bass, we decide, biopsied
out & the pond's feeder stream insinuating

liquid but meaning only weak hormonal
dribble where it has enough flow to be

a symbol. 5 AM—the pond is already lost
in Crawford's penciled directions, in his neural

map. We drive dark roads. We see
in pieces: a farm ruin we are suddenly

in the middle of as gravel pops
in our fenders & the car slides, the farm

an idyll, a presumption, an ingenuous
arguing for our species, the farm's abandoned

hop frames, the wire cagework our lights
articulate as we pass, as we shudder & grind

back into tree outlines or low brush,
continuing. 4 AM—we load the car at city's

edge. We can have our fish yet. The pond
is not yet tainted by irony. Crawford will sing

as he drives. How real the fish seem
when we talk bait!

Rivers

Carried along by things—
Charlotte's bad eyes, in-laws, the instants

of sexual transport, school do's—
any series starts a river.

In nature, the trickle under a culvert
you stoop to go in, shoes absorbing.

Swing-clink & cries from the asphalted
playground are back there—

it's suburban but Chicago—
around you, ailanthus & the crawlholes

kids use. You wet your face,
you splash maps onto your shirt.

*

In its own Forest
Preserve, the Chicago-choked Des Plaines

spreads a few steps wide. It's stew-brown
from spring flood, elm & bramble mush

nudged by counter-currents until the daubwork
ripples meet—*downstream* is what a river says.

On the Mississippi at Night

Not anchored to anything, we drift
between polarities—Iowa equal

to Illinois—pulled by the surface
we slide on, pulled the same, we think,

by Antares or our own atoms,
our skiff a clutter of gear we feel

more than see, our Coleman lantern's
reflection shiny as a tongue-stud

in the current. We'd intended
the inconsequential catfish & got bug-bites—

no-see-ums & mosquitoes that we breathed
in, breathing out canned repellents our bodies

had not evolved enough to make.
We'd intended slough, & now, motor up,

Crawford, one foot out in mud, pushing,
we're into the quibble of little creeks,

waste drains, & noble tributaries,
all of the participant watershed, then out

into the concepts *Upper Devonian Sea*
& *continental drift*. Open river—damned to any

elision in the humid dark, any evolutionary debt—
mother's father's bad eyes, eczema, floating

debris, all the *insteads* & their parodies, Ernst's German
bride lost (1878) Ellis Island. But what else

did we lose: stink bait first & the dog-paddle,
a pageantry of civilizations reduced to lit-up Dubuque

& across the river's mile of dark, East Dubuque.
Crawford drags an oar, which turns us to Iowa in

a slow spin; with a Crawford whisper & chuckle,
he oar-spins us to Illinois, pulling up his cooling six-pack

like a last anchor.

Ishmael

The critic who called him all *moby*
& no *dick* misunderstood Ishmael's role

six degrees of separation removed from
Ahab. We set out in whaleboats, cursing

the book's long-windedness, coming back
to the *Pequod* sun-burned, our palms bloody.

I learned to row cursing whales in the Iowa
slough locals called Lake Peosta, my oars

stirring scum, stirring its dense subtext.
There, my first fishhook & my dad rust

together but forty years apart—the hook
dug out at that time from my adolescent scalp,

the father dug again & again from the same
but older head to gain forgiveness.

I was my father's Ishmael—wouldn't touch
stinkbait, couldn't boat caught fish & hooked

only myself in a cast that almost overturned
the small skiff as I stood abruptly, & my dad,

his foot down in water to steady the skiff,
losing forever his saved-for Fenwick rod.

The belief in pain is itself the threshold to pain—
I cried as he cut leader & hook-shank both,

kneading the barb out through my skin, his face,
as I watched it, like a soft fruit impressed

with the fingers that picked it.

Rio Vista

Mid-March, the striped bass ease
past Rio under the chop, the currents

that wrap sand like smoke around
the bridge piers. Locals don't mind wind

contrary to the tide, or the heavy
rented skiffs that fish inside theirs.

Late afternoon they will scratch
a few keepers from the sandbar

with a pop-eyed jig or Rebel
trolled shallow. By June the spawned-

out fish will ride downriver again.
Gulls again patrol for boat garbage

over the launches, ignoring
Coors & Oly cans that clunk & clunk

the floats. Wet to the elbows, the same
old woman who stopped you

for a sandwich on your way out,
kneels to snag the redeemable

empties, steps them flat.

Port Townsend

Two deer alike as clones stop
at the curb, the steep stair

to the four-room Carnegie Library
behind them as though they'd come

down benumbed by a former
life in books. The day that had changed

with them is downhill,
its color beaten to the undersides

of clouds, the sun low & thwarted
as the animals might be

by outwaiting our stopped human traffic
that also waits to see them

cross (ironically) to the closed realty
office: a village has little turnover

in housing, no industry & few plans.
I make theocracies in my car, complain

the deer are not Ovid's godlings.
Peninsular Washington's a forest

cut into cottages or Asia's pulp.
I look downhill, almost to Asia

for traffic answers, the car throbbing
as though it too looks

into a future solely of cars & instrument
gleam, not this line of streetlamps

punctuating human tasks, deer exits.
One deer is a locution,

but two confirm the indrawn Biblical
breath that will make a world fecund.

Both animals turn, surely not in scorn
of us, but not denying attraction either,

their thin legs scissoring them
back up the Library steps to the pre-literate

& Edenic sideyard, dark with rhododendron.

The Last Ferry from Whidbey Island: My 65th Birthday

Nineteen nights straight my walk's here
where I can imagine lit Seattle,

heaped-up glass & mixed-bloods metal,
a species wink-out only an hour away under

the horizon east. I'm bundled for the long
wet wait in Gore-Tex & memory layers

you'd mock but wear too.
The incoming ferry's momentum

a destiny now, the dock timbers grunt
then ping arpeggios some gulls echo

tonight as they furl then open
gladly to eat on wing

the last popcorn two girls on the upper deck
discard. The ramp of years I'm on angles

down—almost underfoot,
gray Xeroxed waves, shuffled & re-shuffled,

dog-ear off the prow. If I'm in danger,
it's not the preemptive green

& white hull I can't see over
or around as it swings limitless

mass, & a deckhand far overhead curses
down. Danger's only emotive conditioning—

if I'd dare reach to touch the pattern
of rivets, I'd realize that it's only metal

gooseflesh & laugh.

Binoculars

Paradoxically, glasses make the scene
more remote—the distance even slows

thought, until the gull above me,
spirit of the place, screams, sings as
it hangs, its held note uneroded though

the weather blows. The gull's a survivor
who sings into the squall a second-hand
grief I'm never asked to join, waves

that churn then level a tire-marked beach.
A sandpiper downwind dips into the wet
sand at the seam between two worlds.

I can't see where the ocean comes apart
because of the turbulence, because of
the existential blindness the binoculars posit

in positing distance. The dory upwind
is the test her amateur crew, counterstressed
by motive, fails. They fight fifteen minutes

to right her, broadside against the power
of the ocean, winch her into this world—
one man at the inadequate crank,

another already revving the jeep,
the third simulating anger, his curses blown
back into his mouth before he can turn away.

Natural Selection

Point Reyes: the trail all switchbacks
& pebbly, & suddenly, a coyote which is eating

someone's sandwich, not yet someone,
the sandwich wrapper dangling from its grin—

far below us, the Pacific is sun-bit & restless
as chain-mail.

Kansas City: again running, but in my host's
borrowed Adidas & thinking blisters,
belly-flesh swaying—without meaning to,

I'm running to come in last. Two lanes
forward to Kansas, two lanes back to Missouri,
beside me skinny Bush Creek toiling
through sumac—even bumper to bumper,

the drivers in vendetta. We all are running
for humans to come in last—to make room
for us, the species ahead sidesteps into extinction,

a new species every nine minutes, one every
five years in Darwin's time. The spider tortoise's
too-short legs, the easily-distracted & slow tree boa.

What's ahead & stops us on Bush Creek Blvd
is ad hoc—signs & slogans against road-kill.
A few adults & some kids hand us flattened-

animal-shaped cookies iced in pink
tire-tread. One kid has painted black tread
across his face & down his shirtfront.

Their dogs & pets in an uneasy bunch mill
around them. It is (momentarily) enough.

Ad Hoc

Those days, Vietnam & little money.
Those days, in the tool-shed hutch outback,

the upstairs neighbor's rabbit ate whatever
bedding-newspaper stuck to kitchen

scraps. Call this last uneaten rabbit *ad hoc*,
when rabbits begin to mean,

when the only food in the cupboard is reduced
to smell. Next call an *ad hoc* light down

on any quote of thorazine-rich gospel
that keeps the neighbor believing at the window

above the place where he'd parked the VW bus
he didn't want repossessed. He was an hour

in camouflage, he told me, an hour in the plastic
drapes he had knotted closed to an *ad hoc* eye-peek,

shivering because the space heater sighed
out in Wisconsin cold, its valve choked,

& fuel a wind-blown block to the Mobil
station or a whiff in the kerosene can he shook

a magic three times, cursing snow.
He said he'd prayed for an *ad hoc* wind

to keep the VW's door an imperfectly-shut
deterrent for the key he had left ringless

in the ignition, the crushed Coke cans,
the Nixon mask summer had half-melted in

the glove-box. 5 AM, he'd prayed for the snowplow
that would seal the street, half-bury the bus.

Birds

All day I fix the birds;
the nails come bent

the old holes open—
the one for song & the one

for dung.
The next man can glue lips

to kisses. The next man can
put wings to despair.

On the eye bush, the last eye
opens, swimming

with winter pictures.
I hang up the shears & bend

close to watch
shadows cross a dark

pupil: birds going south.
Overhead, real birds

return. The gauze net is done
just in time.

A blackbird dives; another
whistles in the tongue tree

out of reach

The light that instinct sheds
is enough though night has doubled

the dimensions of the barn.
Here you have wings, such small wings,

& cry out with the barn swallows
even if you must gag on mud

& make your nest with filthy breath.
The cat in the loft circles around itself

twice then sleeps.

Jewels

Today, my father's watch is first
out of her therapist's box, next brooch, then thimble—
though my mother cries, it's the order

not the sentimental cachet her therapist
tests. Last week, my mother didn't remember
the ten test words the therapist also used

in sentences. Today, my mother's First Communion
holy-card comes out last, & when she turns it
over to share its drama, its children are no farther

up the mountain they ascend, gravel biting
the bare feet they dig with going up so high
that these illustrated crows are eye-level.

Down on the card's earth, the tail
of the lizard that is Satan is what the children's
bare feet touched to make the first step

heavenward. From the Castle at the blue's
top edge, a saint shovels jewels
into the gravel, or is that the gravel's meaning

only found by the feet as the child toils higher?

Elms

I'm not sleeping really in my former
home but sleeping in my self until

the Iowa in me—or one street, my street,
leads me, longing, to the older body's

morning. It's my brother's house now.
This would've been my bedroom window

in which the wind is all verb, & sun,
finite but in a thousand leaves,

flicks & flicks. Eat, my brother urges,
then walk, & so we walk still negotiating

our fit—where he's monosyllabic, I perfect,
disappointed as we go, a lower-case praise

of trees, the neighborhood's necrotic Dutch
elm victims, scions dying on the warty galls.

Praise the blurt & syncopated chirr of chain
saws: the City's culling what I was bred for—

I am metaphorically cut but not cut down,
happy just to be, sixty-five but still

preliminary. Now our walk is transaction,
board-game rules: one step back, two steps

into complicity as the crew-chief signals
our way through the downed trees, prone trunks,

really just torsos, limbs gnawed arm-length
& then all into the rusted truck-bed,

a coarse spew that blows back on two workers
who feed the chipper. Chuang Tzu's wise man

is just a tree that grow big because its trunk
is too twisted for coffin-lids, leaves

poisonous when the disciple licked one.
The crew-chief's face is clamped in a parenthesis

his ear-protectors make, a moral deafness—
are the saws so loud that he can't hear the trees

scream? We walk on. What used to be is knotted
in the roots of what is, the bedroom's

sick elm where sun once flooded my childhood.

Acknowledgments

Grateful acknowledgment to the editors who published these poems, a few in earlier versions:

Caliban: "Phone Calls"
Chicago Review: "The Woods," "Port Townsend," "The Last Ferry from Whidbey Island," "Rio Vista"
Cincinnati Review: "On the Mercator Map," "Ishmael"
Drumvoices: "My Grandfather's Gambol"
FIELD: "Animism," "Boundaries We Don't See," "Bait," "On the Mississippi at Night," "Birds" (sections one and two), "Talking into the Monster's Hat," "Song of Myself," "Thirteen," "Our Place"
Great River Review: "Accidents & Effects," "Ad Hoc"
The Iowa Review: "Bird-Talk," "Heckfire," "Yellowjackets," "Rivers"
The Journal: "Doppelganger"
Michigan Quarterly Review: "Listening to Pan," "Film Noir"
Northwest Review: "Brand Loyalty"
Plum: "Picking Blackberries"
Poetry: "Intimacy," "Elms"
Poetry Now: "Dungeon—Sutter's Fort, CA"

The FIELD Poetry Series